Praise for Barbara Rubel's *But I L*

"SA\VE applauds the honesty ~~and accuracy of this book.~~ At long last an author tells the truth to children about the cause of suicide. The words depression, disease, chemical imbalance in the brain are music to the ears of suicide prevention advocates working to erase centuries of ignorance. Even the use of the word 'completed' rather 'committed' suicide shows insight into the long process that results in suicide."

-Mary Kluesner,
President, SA\VE, Suicide Awareness\Voices of Education

"The heartbroken questing of Alex in *But I Didn't Say Goodbye* echo the fear, the struggle to understand, the need for reassurance and comfort by children bereaved by suicide everywhere. *But I Didn't Say Goodbye* responds to Alex's questions of suicide, confident of promoting the child's healthy grief resolution and laying a sound foundation for the child's future well-being."

-LaRita Archibald,
HEARTBEAT
Support in the Aftermath of Suicide

"As someone who as a child lost his father to suicide, I warmly recommend Barbara Rubel's book. It will help young suicide survivors deal with the bafflement, sense of abandonment, and depression that are so often the sad legacies of suicide. Rubel suggests how the child can discover some meaning in an act that often seems to erode meaning and value, and how the child can begin to cope with and surmount a tragedy that will, in some respects, be with him or her for a lifetime."

-Larry Lockridge,
Professor of English, New York University,
author, *Shade of the Raintree: The Life and Death of Ross Lockridge, Jr.,*
author of *Raintree County*

"*But I Didn't Say Goodbye* is clearly outlined. It not only tells us who the book is for, but how they can use it. The author, Barbara Rubel begins by telling her own story, the suicide of her father. The book is as much a need to educate us, as her need for healing. Of course, that is the key to any good survivors book in the field.

What allows this book to resonate to us is the actual verbalizations of Alex, a young boy faced with the unfaceable; His daddy's suicide. Barbara Rubel guides us through the questions, blames, issues . . . and PAIN of a young person. It does so through the actual protocols of Alex - of course, narrative accounts have always been richer than just words. Suicide notes are a good example. One can feel the boy's pain . . . the protocols do justice to the rich individuality of each of us, something that no statistical, scientific report can. It provides us with the ideographic approach that has been central to suicidology since Shneidman and Farberow's 1957 monumental book, *Clues to Suicide*.

Alex's protocols not only allow us to understand this young boy's aftershocks but also provide a guide for us to help - Alex's dialogues with his mother, uncle, grandparent, coach, show us direction. It shows a basic fact in postvention. Everyone can help in the healing process. Indeed, it takes the community to help our Alexs'.

As a final guidance, Barbara Rubel in her book presents the ultimate healing to quote Alex's grandmother, 'I love you Alex.' Eros can do wonders in our life."

-Antoon A. Leenaars,
Psychotherapy, Consultation, Research and Specialized Workshops
Windsor, Ontario Canada

But
I Didn't
Say
Goodbye

But
I Didn't
Say
Goodbye

For parents
and professionals
helping child suicide survivors

Barbara Rubel

Griefwork Center, Inc.   New Jersey

Distributed in the U.S.A. by Griefwork Center, Inc.
P.O. Box 5104
Kendall Park, New Jersey 08824

ISBN 1-892906-00-7
Library of Congress Catalog Card Number 99-96975

To order book or for information about Barbara Rubel's availability for workshops, presentations, and training contact:
Barbara Rubel
Griefwork Center, Inc.
P.O. Box 5104
Kendall Park, NJ 08824
732-422-0400   Fax 732-422-4609
e-mail: Griefworkpress@aol.com
Web site: http://www.Griefworkcenter.com

ATTENTION ORGANIZATIONS AND SCHOOLS

Quantity discounts are available on bulk purchases of this book for educational purposes or fund raising. For information, please contact Griefwork Center, Inc., P.O. Box 5104, Kendall Park, NJ 08824 or call 732-422-0400 / fax 732-422-4609.

For my children, Alan, Matthew, Michael and Brian.
When your grandfather completed suicide,
you became survivors.
In becoming survivors, you became my greatest teachers.
You have taught me that bonds are never severed.
Your voice reaches into my soul and
touches the memory of my father.
I carry his memory,
and you, my dear sons, carry his legacy.

CONTENTS

Part of the proceeds of this book will be donated to
the Association for Death Education and Counseling
and the American Foundation for Suicide Prevention

ACKNOWLEDGMENTS

From the time I first decided to write *But I Didn't Say Goodbye*, through its many drafts, I have been blessed with the encouragement of many talented people. They were helpful in integral ways, reading this work in manuscript form, offering helpful, constructive comments, or giving examples from their own experience. Although I list them together, each person's contribution is individually appreciated, Edward I. Paley, Joy Johnson, Lori Koppelman, Sharamee Kerr, Jerine Watson, Frank Campbell, Myra Morrant, Donna Schurrman, Debbi Dickinson, Sidney Pech, Eileen Glaser, Marilyn Koenig, Mary J. Kluesner, and Jeri Dinneen. My deepest thanks to Ben Wolfe, who shared so much of his gentle wisdom from a cabin in the woods of Northern Minnesota. My thanks to David Meagher, Brooklyn College, Department of Health and Nutritional Sciences, Thanatology Program, who has educated and empowered me in my work with the bereaved.

To Charlie Castaldo, I treasure our friendship. I'm thankful for the friendship of Mindy Swid and Mary Parisi. My gratitude to Debbie Goldsmith, for her positive energy and enthusiasm for my ambitions. Heartfelt thanks to those who attend the SOLAS group, and to the grieving children, who are the seed inspiration for many of the insights contained in this book.

My loving husband, Robert, who is a continued and cherished source of support, and without whom, this book could never have been possible. My mother, Ida Greenwald, whose love is boundless. Arnold and Ellen Greenwald, Betty and Lenny Rubel, Denise and Ivan Rubel, and Arlene and Steven Schneier for their ongoing support of this project.

ABOUT THE AUTHOR

Barbara Rubel is a nationally known consultant to mental health organizations, school systems, business, and parent groups across the United States. Ms. Rubel specializes in suicide survivor bereavement and has been working for the past twelve years developing her Caregivers Responding In Situations Involving Suicide (C.R.I.S.I.S.) Model. Barbara has appeared on television, radio and is widely published. Through her workshops, in-service trainings, and literature, she has reached millions who want to understand the unique and intensified grief of suicide survivors.

Barbara received her B.S. in Psychology and is a MA candidate in Community Health with Thanatology concentration. She also has a Certificate of Advance Study in The Skilled Helper, an intensive Bereavement Training Program in personal and technical skills of Bereavement Care Giving on the issues of Complicated Mourning. Ms. Rubel is a Certified Pastoral Bereavement Counselor and is a Certified Bereavement Specialist.

Three weeks prior to Barbara's giving birth to triplets, her father, a retired New York City police officer, took his own life. Barbara's story is featured in a 1998 PBS documentary, Fatal Mistakes: Families Shattered by Suicide, narrated by Mariette Hartley. This full-length, Emmy award winning television documentary educates viewers about suicide's impact on survivors and the latest advances in prevention.

Since 1995, Barbara has been facilitating a monthly suicide survivor support group, SOLAS, Sharing Our loss After Suicide, at St. Francis Medical Center in Trenton, New Jersey. Ms. Rubel serves on the New Jersey Affiliate of the American Foundation for Suicide Prevention. Her current research interests focus on the image of suicide in the media and public awareness. As a suicide survivor and as a mother of four sons, Barbara understands how important it is to speak to children honestly about suicide. This book, born out of her own personal tragedy, is the first in a series utilizing the Caregivers Responding In Situations Involving Suicide (C.R.I.S.I.S.) Model.

INTRODUCTION

HOW THIS BOOK IS ORGANIZED

THE INTRODUCTION includes how this book is organized, how to read this book, who should read this book, a note to the professional, and a note to the parent. This book is for the helping professional or parent as you try to help children in the aftermath of suicide.

   PART ONE presents Alex, a ten-year-old whose father has just died by suicide. Alex asks questions and tries to find meaning in the loss. At the end of each chapter in Part One, there are pages with STOP signs. The purpose of the eight Stop to Process pages is to help the grieving child process his or her own story.

   PART TWO offers information on setting up a Memorial Fund, and will help in your search for prevention and survivor support. As a caregiver, it is important to seek out organizations that help you help survivors. To keep suicide survivor support group information updated, a toll-free number is given for groups in your area. Bereavement referrals include death education and grief counseling organizations, crisis intervention, information on addictions and depression, and camps for grieving children.

   APPENDIX A includes recommended resources, bereavement magazines, newsletter, reports, journals, books and articles. Find videos, tapes, and a reading list that will help you continue your exploration of suicide awareness, prevention and bereavement.

HOW TO READ THIS BOOK

A child survivor of suicide is one whose family member or friend took his or her own life. As you are brought into that child's world, you will use the character, ten-year-old, Alex, as a frame of reference to reach the specific issues troubling the child you are helping. Pre-adolescent children are aware of the finality of death. However, children don't have the maturity to cope with grief alone. At this age, they can recognize the possibility of their own deaths and they can feel overwhelmed by stress and anxiety.

Children shouldn't read Alex's story by themselves and it's recommended that you read it first yourself. Share Alex's story with the child and listen to the child. Read each chapter and explore the questions that unfold. Alex's questions are the same as many other child suicide survivors. However, every child is unique and adults do not always have the answers. Provide loving reassurance while respecting the child's questions and silence as the child tries to assimilate their turbulent thoughts. Try to tune in to the feelings behind the question, though "you" may also be a survivor and grieving too. As you know, this is an unbelievably difficult time for everyone. If you are reading this book with a child, do so at their pace. Use this book in a way that works for you!

Utilizing the Caregivers Responding In Situations Involving Suicide (C.R.I.S.I.S.) Model, the dialogue in each short chapter will show you how you can help develop honest, open communication between the child suicide survivor and the people in his or her life. In Part One, (Chapters 1 - 9), the child's needs in the aftermath of suicide are explored. Chapter 1, The Worst Day, focuses on how to tell a child that someone they cared about completed suicide. Chapter 2, My Hidden Thoughts, identifies the child's thoughts as they search for answers. Chapter 3, Mom Tries to Explain Why, poignantly illustrates how to talk about mental illness with a child. Chapter 4, Grandma's Special Gift, shows the significance of giving the child a special object that belonged to the deceased. Chapter 5, the Next Morning, deals with the child's grief response. Chapter 6, Lunch with Coach, examines past losses. Chapter 7, Telling a Friend What Happened, explores the importance of sharing one's story. Chapter 8, Finding

Support, focuses on the benefit of Bereavement Counselors and support groups for children. Chapter 9, A Note from Alex, is a summary of the continuing attachment between Alex and his dad.

 In Part One, there are Stop to Process pages with STOP Signs. *Stop* reading Alex's story and *Start* exploring the questions and activities listed with the child you're helping. Stop to Process pages offers questions for children to reflect upon and will help them process their own story. Use them as client handouts.

In Part Two and Appendix A, you will find what a caregiver needs to know when helping suicide survivors. See referrals in Part Two and resources in Appendix A. The C.R.I.S.I.S. Model incorporates resources and referrals as a major part of the healing process in the aftermath of suicide. It promotes the involvement of survivors in prevention programs. Rather than help the suicide survivor on your own, the emphasis should be on seeking out the support of organizations dedicated to prevention, intervention and healing.

WHO SHOULD USE THIS BOOK

Though this book reaches out to those helping child suicide survivors, it is a book for everyone touched by suicide. *But I Didn't Say Goodbye* is an innovative approach to the sensitive and challenging task facing bereavement counselors, social workers, psychologists, nurses, funeral home aftercare personnel, clergy, educators, parents and media. *But I Didn't Say Goodbye* is to help you, the professional and parent, explore how children cope with the trauma of suicide. Take an in-depth look through a child's eyes, at the first and terribly painful days following a suicide.

A NOTE TO THE PROFESSIONAL

But I Didn't Say Goodbye can help unlock the child's feelings of abandonment, loss, and social stigma. Begin working with child survivors as soon as possible after the suicide. The violent separation between the child and the person who died is extremely difficult. The words you use to talk about suicide with a child, are your own. Find what is comfortable for you. As a helping professional, your words will provide child survivors a safe place to share their story.

In my story, Alex's father suffered from clinical depression. It's important to share with the child that not all people who are clinically depressed die by suicide. There is no one reason why someone completes suicide. Scientists are now studying low serotonin and biochemistry in the brain and are learning about the complexity of suicide. Being aware of family history of suicide is a factor in preventing future suicides within that same family. Though you are helping the child suicide survivor, your work will no doubt intimately affect every family member. The entire family has been shaken to its very core.

The child may be reluctant to talk about the suicide. Hoping to change the language to avoid the stigma, "completed suicide" is used, rather than committed suicide. Shame and a social stigma may cloud the truth if the child's family has not been completely honest about the details. The child needs someone they can rely on for honest answers. Answers should be based on their age and developmental level.

In looking at suicide as a public health problem, personality, coping skills, past loss history, gender, religion, sexual orientation, and cultural background are important factors to consider. Perceive how the suicide occurred and the depth of their relationship. They may be self medicating by alcohol or drugs. Ask whether any of their friends completed or attempted suicide. Find out whether the child found the person who died and whether they witnessed the suicide. Behavioral and emotional needs, somatic responses, and any school-based problems should be addressed. Children may experience denial, poor peer relations, or aggressiveness and may be experiencing post-traumatic shock as they face the unexpected and seemingly insurmountable problems that turned their lives upside down.

Adult survivors in the child's life have their own means of coping with sudden and sometimes violent death. Many find comfort through friend and family support, faith, support groups, professional counseling or staying busy. Actively finding ways to cope during this difficult time, such as reading, *But I Didn't Say Goodbye*, will help them during this crisis. Though you are a helping provider, you may be struggling with your own questions about death and suicide. Hopefully, this book will help you understand your own feelings about suicide.

A NOTE TO THE PARENT

When I was in labor giving birth to my triplet sons, my beloved father took his own life. I was traumatized by this horror, this unbelievable loss, and at the same time torn between the utter joy of having three healthy babies and the grief of knowing their grandfather would never hold them close or know them as they grew up. And they would never know their grandfather.

I was very close to my father. He was always there for me, always accepting of me, always supportive and loving. He was my rock, my history, my background, my heritage. He was part of my life, a part I had taken for granted and that I believed would always be there.

As the days passed, my grief seemed to have no cessation in sight. I would do things automatically, like a robot, and then without warning, the overwhelming fact of my father's suicide would fall in on me like a mile-high wall of bricks. I felt like I was going forward two steps at a time and falling backward a dozen. There was so much to take care of with triplets. But there always came the moment when the loss would surface. And the truth kept screaming at me, "I never got to tell my father goodbye!"

Why? I kept asking the empty space in my heart, where he used to be. Why did you do this terrible thing to us, who loved you so? Why didn't you ask for help from somebody? Why didn't we see it coming? Why didn't you at least wait until you saw the babies? Why? Why? Why? A million times I wept and asked this unanswerable question.

The main things I have tried to stress in *But I Didn't Say Goodbye* are compassion, understanding, patience and acceptance of the survivor's need to ask questions, to talk about his or her feelings. There were times when my children would ask me a question about my dad's suicide and I simply did not know what to say. I have always given them answers as best I could. When I did not have the words, I hugged them, and that brought comfort to us both. And now I have written this book for those who are helping child suicide survivors with their questions.

As I grieved the death of my father, my body, mind and spirit were affected by the loss. Searching for meaning in his loss, in his suicide, and meaning in my own life, I attended a suicide survivor support group and found it to be a great help. I then started a support group in my area and continue to facilitate the group that meets monthly at a local hospital. I named the group SOLAS, which means Sharing Our Loss After Suicide. The sharing of stories helped me deal with my grief. I also read books on suicide as I was searching for answers. Attending suicide survivor conferences, and becoming active in prevention programs were ways I dealt with the tragedy of my dad's death. I found ways to help me heal and have included many of the resources in this book that have helped me on my own journey as a survivor.

I was attached to my dad and his death affected me spiritually. I have evolved from a place where I could not forgive my dad for taking his life to a place where I accommodated the experience of his suicide into my life and found meaning in it. My aspiration is that you will walk away from *But I Didn't Say Goodbye* inspired and motivated to do something incredibly powerful and enriching - and that is to help a child suicide survivor find meaning in the loss. I hope in some small way, my thoughts can help you achieve your goals.

PART ONE

The Big Questions

1

THE WORST DAY

Hi, my name is Alex. Five years ago, when I was ten years old and in the fifth grade, my dad died by suicide. He killed himself while I was at school. It was very cold that morning, so I put on my coat and got my book bag and my lunch and walked right by my dad. He was sitting at the kitchen table with my mom, reading the newspaper and drinking his coffee, just like he did every morning. My five-year-old sister, Debbie, was eating cereal as she watched TV. I was late so I ran out the door and down the street to the bus stop.

I always take the bus home, but that day, my uncle Sammy picked me up early from school. He never picked me up before, so I asked him why he was there. He said that we would talk about it when we got home. We drove up to the house and there were a few cars parked outside. My mom was sitting on the couch and there were people with her. She looked really sad. Her face was all puffy and her eyes were red. When she saw me, she gave me a big hug and we walked into my room where we sat on the bed together. She was having a hard time telling me something.

What happened, Mom?
Alex, Daddy completed suicide this morning. Completed suicide means he killed himself.

Why did Daddy kill himself?
I keep asking myself the same question, Alex. He had some serious problems. We aren't sure what all the problems were.

How did he do it?
Daddy shot himself with his gun.

No! I don't believe you! Is this a joke?
No joke. It really happened.

Was anybody there when he did it?
No, Dad was by himself. I found his body in the basement.

I wondered if I'd ever want to go into the basement again. I started to think about Dad and the gun. The gun probably made a loud noise. I think he died very fast. I bet my dad was scared. I almost couldn't say what I thought of next.

Mom, did he kill himself because of something I said or did?
You're feeling worried that you're to blame. Nothing you said or did or thought made Dad kill himself. But, let's talk about what you're feeling. He loved you very much.

Mom and I cried while we talked. I didn't cry very hard, though. It didn't seem real yet and I was so confused. I couldn't believe that my dad was dead. It was a shock.

Stop to Process

WHEN DID I HEAR ABOUT THE DEATH OF MY SPECIAL PERSON?

WHO TOLD ME THAT MY SPECIAL PERSON WAS DEAD?

HOW DID I FEEL WHEN I WAS TOLD ABOUT THE DEATH?

WHERE WAS I WHEN MY SPECIAL PERSON DIED?

HOW DO I FEEL ABOUT THE PERSON WHO TOLD ME THAT MY SPECIAL PERSON DIED?

WHAT DO I THINK HAPPENED AT THE TIME OF MY SPECIAL SOMEONE'S DEATH?

WHAT HAPPENED WHEN I HEARD THE WORD DEAD?

WHAT DOES THE DEATH OF MY SPECIAL PERSON MEAN TO ME?

MAKE A LIST OF FACTS I KNOW ABOUT DEATH.

HOW DOES THE WORD SUICIDE MAKE ME FEEL?

DRAW A PICTURE OF THE DAY I WAS TOLD ABOUT THE DEATH.

2

MY HIDDEN THOUGHTS

My dad's older brother, Uncle Sammy, was looking through our photo album and he had tears in his eyes. It felt scary to see Uncle Sammy like that. I thought about the times my dad and I would put new pictures in the album. My dad would sit in his favorite chair and I would hand him the pictures. It was fun. Now, my uncle was sitting in my dad's favorite chair and that made me miss my dad even more. I talked to my uncle about what I was thinking and he made me feel like what I had to say was important. He didn't ignore me because I was a kid.

Uncle Sammy, I keep thinking my dad will walk in the door. I can't stop thinking about him.
I'm thinking about your dad, too. We all miss him and have special memories of him that we'll have as long as we live. What are you thinking about?

I was thinking about school. Dad told me he was going to watch me in my school play next week. Dads aren't

supposed to die! Uncle Sammy, I'm so confused.
When someone you love dies, it hurts more than anything ever hurt before. You can be angry or sad or confused. It just doesn't make sense.

I thought that maybe it wouldn't have happened if I'd been there or if I'd been better or nicer or cleaned my room. But my uncle told me that it wasn't my fault. My dad had big problems. I just never thought that anyone could have problems that big. Suicide changes everything. I was starting to worry about things I never thought of before.

Uncle Sammy, is anyone in our family going to jail?
No, Alex. Your dad didn't break any law. The police came to your home because they needed to talk to your mom about your dad.

I wonder if they thought it was our fault?
No, they blame no one. They know that he used his own gun to end his life. No one ever thought he would use it on himself.

Stop to Process

WHAT AM I THINKING ABOUT RIGHT NOW?

HOW DOES IT FEEL TO HAVE THESE THOUGHTS?

WHO CAN I TALK TO ABOUT THESE THOUGHTS?

MAKE A LIST OF THINGS THAT I WORRIED ABOUT AFTER
THE SUICIDE.

DID ANYONE IN MY FAMILY WORRY ABOUT THE SAME
THINGS I DID?

DRAW A PICTURE OF WHAT I AM WORRYING ABOUT
NOW.

WHERE DO I FEEL SAFE?

I THINK I FEEL SAFE THERE BECAUSE . . .

3

MOM TRIES TO EXPLAIN WHY

My mom was on the phone with my dad's doctor. After she hung up, she sat down with me and my uncle. She said that the doctor told her that everybodys brain has chemicals in it. My dad's brain chemicals were unbalanced. That really confused me. She said that Dad's doctor was treating him for depression. I didn't understand what that meant either. I guess that meant the doctor was trying to make my dad better.

Mom, why didn't the doctor help Dad?
He did try to help Dad. Dad had a serious disease called depression. People have all types of diseases. Those diseases, like depression, are treated by doctors and sometimes those people die, too.

What if I get the same disease as Dad?
Sometimes diseases run in families, but there are new medications being discovered all the time that do a good job in treating these illnesses. Most people who live with depression find relief. I think that Dad didn't believe that he could get better.

9

I wish he could have gotten better.
Me too! Dad wasn't eating well and was drinking a lot of alcohol lately.

I know Mom. It was scary. Dad had problems.
We all have problems. We have to learn how to cope with them and find help if we're having trouble handling them. Dad didn't see any solution to his problems and couldn't cope. Brain disorders can be treated. It is so sad that Dad felt hopeless.

Hopeless?
Uh-huh. He hurt really bad inside. Though most people do get through the emotional pain, I think that Dad believed that he would have an unhappy future.

Am I going to die by suicide too?
No, you are not going to die by suicide. If you ever felt that way, know that there are people who can be with you during that time. Suicide is never the right option.

I'm scared that you're going to die, too! Have you ever felt hopeless, Mom?
No, Alex. It sounds like you're afraid something will happen to me. I am going to try to be as healthy as I can be.

But, you're so sad, Mom.
There may be times when I'm sad because I miss Dad. I don't want you to confuse that with feeling hopeless. A person can be sad, like when someone they love dies.

My mom answered my questions, but I could see that she was sad and was acting differently. We talked about our feelings and she told me that it's normal to act differently when someone you love dies. Sometimes when we talked about my dad, she couldn't stop crying. That really scared me. But, I always felt safe when my mom hugged me.

Stop to Process

HOW HAS THE DEATH OF THE PERSON I CARED ABOUT AFFECTED ME?

WHAT CHANGES HAVE OCCURRED AT MY HOME SINCE THE DEATH?

HOW HAVE PEOPLE IN MY FAMILY CHANGED SINCE MY SPECIAL PERSON DIED?

DRAW A PICTURE OF SOMEONE THAT CARES ABOUT ME.

DRAW A PICTURE OF WHAT I AM FEELING NOW.

4

GRANDMA'S SPECIAL GIFT

My dad's parents slept over that night. Grandma heard me and came to my room. I didn't want to upset her or Mom anymore than they already were, so I thought I should hide my feelings. But Grandma said sharing my feelings with her and Mom was important for all of us.

Grandma, what if I have a nightmare about daddy?
Nightmares are confusing and scary. Even though nightmares are scary, your room is a safe place. Alex, look around your room. All your things are here with you. If you have a dream about Daddy, good or bad, we'll find the time to talk about it.

Grandma, are you wearing Dad's watch?
Yes, I am. Your mom said I could wear it. It feels good wearing something that belonged to your dad. You can wear something that belonged to him, too, like his T-shirt or baseball cap.

Grandma kept touching the watch. I told her that I wanted to wear my dad's baseball cap. She gave me his cap later that night. It was a little big, but I didn't care. It felt good wearing it. I told my grandma that I liked talking to her but didn't want to talk about my dad's death with my friends, my team, no one! My grandma talked with me about secrets. She said that it sounded to her like I wanted to keep my dad's death a secret. She said that he had a disease. His brain was not thinking clearly. She thought that keeping secrets was not healthy. Whether someone dies by suicide or by diseases like cancer or heart attack, it's not going to be easy to talk about. Grandma said it would be a good thing to talk with people I trusted.

Grandma, can I talk to my teacher about what happened?
Yes. Your mom said that she was going to call your teacher, principal, and guidance counselor and let them know what happened.

Thanks Grandma! I think I'm ready for bed now.
I love you Alex.

Grandma told me that she loved me and that she would help me understand what happened to my dad. It was hard for her because she didn't understand it herself. It was hard for me to believe my dad was really dead. I was confused about death and suicide. Grandma didn't have all the answers and whether she was crying or eating or talking or looking at my dad's pictures, I knew she was there and it felt good. Her idea about having something that belonged to my dad, was a great one. I liked wearing my dad's baseball cap. When I grew up, she was going to give me my dad's watch . . . that was awesome.

Stop to Process

DO I HAVE SOMETHING THAT BELONGED TO MY SPECIAL PERSON? IF SO, DESCRIBE IT.

IF I COULD HAVE ONE ITEM THAT BELONGED TO MY SPECIAL PERSON, WHAT WOULD IT BE?

DRAW A PICTURE OF SOMETHING THAT BELONGED TO MY SPECIAL PERSON.

WHY DOES THE OBJECT HAVE SPECIAL MEANING?

AM I DOING ANYTHING WITH MY SPECIAL PERSON'S OBJECT?

HOW DOES THE OBJECT MAKE ME FEEL CONNECTED TO MY SPECIAL PERSON?

HOW WOULD I FEEL IF THE OBJECT WAS LOST?

5

THE NEXT MORNING

I didn't like the way I felt when I woke up. I had so many things I wanted to say to my dad. I dreamed about him that night. It wasn't scary, but I felt all mixed-up. I wondered if I was always going to feel this way. I heard my mom crying while I was trying to go to sleep and it scared me. I wasn't sure if I should go into her bedroom or not. I didn't know what to do. I heard her scream out that she was angry with my dad. Sometimes I felt angry too.

As I was eating breakfast with my sister, Debbie, she said that she wanted our dad to come back. She thought if she wished real hard, she could make him come back home. Our dad was never coming home. He was going to be dead forever. I told her to draw a picture of him. Then we would show it to our mom and ask her to tape it to the wall. Each time we looked at it we would remember our dad.

Dad was a good artist and Debbie thought she drew just like him. She drew a picture of him and then went outside to play in the snow. She built a snowman that made me think of the ones my dad and I used to make. It felt good to remember things I used to do with him.

All of a sudden, I didn't feel like doing anything and I started to cry. Mom saw me and gave me a hug. She then handed me a small book with blank pages in it. She said that it could be my special place to write or draw how I feel. My mom said that I would always feel connected to my dad and I think she's right.

Mom, I have so much to say to Dad. I wonder if Dad can hear me?
I believe his spirit can hear you. What do you want to say to him?

I want to ask him why he killed himself.
What do you think he would say to you?

Maybe he would say that he was sorry. He would say that he should have stayed alive to be with me. I'm angry that Dad killed himself. Now he won't be here to take me places and spend time with me. I feel so weird.
Where do you feel weird in your body?

My head hurts and I've got a stomach ache. Am I getting sick or something?
No, Alex, you're not sick. Those feelings are normal grief feelings.

What's that?
Grief is when your body and mind try to handle a terrible loss. Everyone has different kinds of grief feelings, and it's okay to have them. I have them too. Feeling mad when someone you love dies is normal. And it's okay to cry.

I won't cry in front of the kids at school. They'll think I'm weird.

You're afraid of what the kids at school might think. Alex, you can cry by yourself or with someone you feel safe, and you can always come to me.

If the kids saw me they might laugh.
It hurts to be teased.

I would hit them really hard if they did tease me.
Hitting is not a good idea when you're angry. Can you think of something else to do when you're angry?

I would walk away from the kids who were teasing me, or maybe tell a teacher. Mom, I want to call out to Dad. I know he can't come home but I want to scream out his name and tell him to please come back.
Alex, let it out. You can scream into a pillow or pound the mattress on your bed as hard as you can with your fists. You can invite some friends to the house or turn the volume up loud as you listen to music. You can even take paper cups, the kind that Dad liked to drink his iced tea out of, and line up a few on the kitchen floor. Then crush them under your sneakers.

Yeah, doing stuff is cool. But, I miss dad so much. I need him so much. How could he leave me like this?
It sounds like you're trying to figure out why Dad killed himself. I know that Dad felt worthless lately. He was anxious all the time and he couldn't concentrate. This is so hard for all of us to understand.

My mom told me that she loved me and hugged me real tight. Her hug felt good even though she was crying. Sometimes I cried too. Sometimes I just felt numb. Sometimes I was scared. Most of all, I was confused.

Mom, lately dad wouldn't play ball with me. I was

confused because he always played with me. The day before he died, I asked him to play ball and he said "No".

He didn't have an interest in anything. Talking about Dad helps us to understand how he felt.

Okay, Mom. Do you think if I had been with him, I could have kept him alive?

Alex, you could have done nothing to save him. You know how much he loved you. His thinking just wasn't right.

I'd always miss my dad but there were things I could do to feel better. Mom told me to draw a picture of where in my body I felt mixed-up, so we could talk about it. I drew a picture of my body with a blue crayon. It was a stick figure. I drew a big red heart on the bottom of the paper. Mom said that my heart looked like it was broken in two. I wondered if Dad could see my drawing and if he knew about my heart. I wondered if he could hear what my mom and I were talking about.

My mom said that she was going to talk to my teacher about what happened. It seemed like everyone knew. The house was filled with people and they were talking about my dad. Without him there, it felt different and strange.

Stop to Process

MAKE A LIST OF THINGS I WOULD LIKED TO HAVE TOLD MY SPECIAL PERSON.

WHO HAVE I ASKED ABOUT WHAT HAPPENS AFTER DEATH?

WHAT DID THEY TELL ME?

WHERE DO I THINK MY SPECIAL PERSON IS NOW?

WHAT CHANGES HAVE I NOTICED IN MY BEHAVIOR SINCE MY SPECIAL PERSON DIED?

DRAW A PICTURE OF MYSELF REALLY ANGRY.

WHAT DO I DO TO CONTROL MY ANGER?

WHAT CHANGES HAVE I NOTICED IN MY BODY SINCE MY SPECIAL PERSON DIED?

DRAW A PICTURE OF THE PLACE IN MY BODY THAT HURTS OR FEELS MIXED-UP.

SINCE THE DEATH, WHAT CHANGES HAVE I NOTICED IN THE PERSON THAT CARES ABOUT ME?

HOW ARE THE CHANGES I MENTIONED THE SAME AS MY OWN CHANGES?

HOW ARE THE CHANGES I MENTIONED DIFFERENT FROM MY OWN CHANGES?

6

LUNCH WITH COACH

It was lunchtime and my stomach started growling. My baseball coach, Charlie, came to see me. We ate pizza and drank orange soda together. I told Charlie that since my dad had always taken me to baseball practice, I was scared I might not get to be a part of the team anymore.

Charlie, my dad always took me to my games. Who's going to take me to my practices and games now?
If your mom says it's okay, I can take you. Would you like that?

Yeah, thanks! There's a game next week. Can you take me to that?
Sure. You don't have to worry about missing any of your practices or any of the games.

Thanks, Coach. I can't believe my dad won't be at my games any more. I keep thinking about that. I'm also thinking about the last time I saw my dad. He was at the kitchen table. I didn't get a chance to say goodbye to him.

Did he say goodbye to you?

No, I was late and ran for the school bus.
There are still ways to say goodbye when someone dies suddenly.
You can write him a goodbye letter. Keep it and read it whenever
you want to. I believe that when someone we care about dies, we
don't say goodbye to them. We say goodbye to what we shared
with them. Your dad will always be a part of you.

I miss him and all the stuff we did together.
Yeah, he was always at your games. I'll miss him too. Alex, you
might want to make a list of your favorite memories of your dad.

**Coach, I'd like to do that. What do you think I should
tell my teammates if they ask why or how my dad
died?**
Why is a very difficult question to answer. You're just learning
the whys yourself. Share what you know, and only if you want to.

**What if the kids at school find out that he died by
suicide, and stare at me?**
That might make you feel uncomfortable. Every kid is different.
Some might stare at you and others will say they're sorry he died.
Your friends may help you catch up with homework, and your
close friends will be glad to see you back at school.

**Do you think the other kids at school will treat me
differently? I don't want them to act weird or
anything.**
I don't know what they'll do. We could talk about it if you like.

**I guess I'll find out sooner or later. My dad died
sooner than I expected him to. No matter how hard
you want someone to come alive again, they can't. I
wasn't ready for my dad to die right now.**
It was a very sad thing to happen. Has anyone you've known died
before?

My cat died last year.
It's sad when a pet dies. Tell me more about how you felt when your cat died.

I felt like I was to blame. I thought I could've done something to keep him alive. I cried. I missed him. That day, my friend asked me over to his house for lunch and I told him I wasn't hungry even though I was. He had a cat and I just didn't want to see it.
What would have happened if you did go to your friend's house?

The cat would have rubbed against my leg. I like his cat, but it would have been hard to play with it when I was sad about my own cat. I did go to his house after a couple of weeks though, and I pet his cat. When I got home, I took a picture of my cat out of the photo album, and put it in a frame on my desk. I kept his stuffed mouse, that I used to dip in catnip. I remember how he'd swat at it and throw it in the air. Sometimes it almost hit the ceiling.
You have some happy memories of your cat. Some of the feelings you are having now about your dad are a lot like the ones you had when your cat died.

I guess! I don't know. All I know is that I'm really confused.
Alex, Let's go for a walk and talk about it.

My Coach put his arm around me and we went for a long walk. Having him to talk to was important to me. I think he really cared about me. Talking to adults I trusted made me feel better. I don't think that they have all the answers, but it felt good knowing that they were trying to understand how I felt. I remember I even laughed when Charlie said something funny. Hearing myself reminded me of my Dad's laugh. We had the same kind of laugh and it felt good to know that.

Stop to Process

WHAT THINGS REMIND ME OF MY SPECIAL PERSON?

DID ANYONE COME TO MY HOUSE AFTER THE SUICIDE?

IF ANYONE CAME TO MY HOUSE, WHAT DID THEY DO OR SAY?

IS THERE ANYTHING THAT MY SPECIAL PERSON USED TO DO FOR ME THAT ANOTHER PERSON IS NOW DOING?

WRITE A LIST OF THINGS YOUNG PEOPLE SAID THAT WERE HELPFUL.

WRITE A LIST OF THINGS YOUNG PEOPLE SAID THAT WERE MEAN.

WHAT QUESTIONS DID MY FRIENDS ASK WHEN THEY FOUND OUT ABOUT THE DEATH?

AM I KEEPING AWAY FROM A PERSON OR PLACE THAT REMINDS ME OF MY SPECIAL PERSON'S DEATH?

WHAT WOULD HAPPEN IF I SPOKE WITH SOMEONE OR WENT TO THE PLACE THAT REMINDS ME OF MY SPECIAL PERSON'S DEATH?

WHAT AM I FEELING RIGHT NOW?

7

TELLING A FRIEND
WHAT HAPPENED

After my coach left, I threw snowballs at my sister's snowman. She made some snowballs, too, and we both hit that snowman really hard. My friend, Steven, walked over to us as we played. At first, I wanted to run back in the house, but I didn't move. Steven said he had been home from school sick and had seen the police car in front of my house. I remember he asked why the police were at my house.

Steven, my dad died while I was at school.
How did he die?

He died by a gunshot.
Was he murdered?

No, he killed himself.
He did? Why?

My mom said that he was in a lot of pain and wasn't thinking right.
Maybe there's been a mistake and maybe he's still alive.

There's been no mistake, even though I feel like it didn't really happen.
What did you do when you first found out?

I felt like all my air had been knocked out of me! I kept asking why. Now I try to think of our good times together and that makes me feel better.
I used to watch you both play ball in the middle of the street. Remember when he taught us how to fly our kites?

Sure. I feel good when I think about the things we did together. I'll miss the way he helped me with my homework. I'll miss the way he said goodnight. Dad always came into my room and tucked me in before I went to sleep. I just don't want to forget him.
You won't forget him. I remember my Cousin Laurie and she died.

Your cousin died?
Uh-huh. She killed herself last year when I was seven. She hung herself.

Why?
I don't know. No one in my family talks about it.

Is it because they're mad at her?
No, I don't think anyone is mad at her. I think they're mad that she killed herself. I don't know because no one talks about her anymore.

Are they keeping it a secret?
No, I don't think so. I don't know. It's confusing.

Yeah. I'm confused too. But, my grandma told me that it's good to talk about our family and friends that have died. No matter if they died by suicide or anything else, it's not a good idea to keep it a secret.

What did you do when you found out your cousin died?
I went out for a walk and I drew a picture of us together. I played with my dog. I also prayed.

Steven, I pray too. Does praying help you?
Uh-huh. I like talking about my cousin. She was cool.

Steven's cousin died by suicide and I think he understood how I was feeling. Later that day, two people came to the house and talked to my mom. I heard my mom say that they understood what she was going through. They were suicide survivors, people whose loved ones died from killing themselves. My mom introduced us as they were talking about support groups for suicide survivors. I noticed that one of the ladies was holding my mom's hand.

Stop to Process

HOW HAS MY RELATIONSHIP WITH THE SPECIAL PERSON WHO DIED CHANGED SINCE THE DEATH?

HOW DO I THINK THE DEATH OF MY SPECIAL SOMEONE MIGHT EFFECT MY FUTURE?

HOW DOES THE WORD SUICIDE MAKE ME FEEL?

MAKE A LIST OF CHANGES IN MY LIFE SINCE MY SPECIAL PERSON DIED.

MAKE A LIST OF REASONS WHY I AM GLAD THAT I AM ALIVE.

WRITE A SPECIAL POEM ABOUT THE PERSON WHO DIED.

DRAW A PICTURE OF WHAT I THINK MY LIFE WILL BE LIKE NEXT YEAR AT THIS TIME.

8

FINDING SUPPORT

My mom told me that she was going to call Joseph, a "bereavement counselor." She said that he talks to kids when someone they love has died.

Mom, what will Joseph ask me?

He'll talk with you about Dad and listen to you. We'll go to his office. You can meet him and talk about the changes in your life since Dad died.

I want to change the way I feel. I want to go back to the way I always felt. Will you go with me?

Your sister and I can go, and we'll talk to him together. He can also find a support group for you.

What's a support group?

It's a group for kids who have had a death in their family.

What will we do when we get together?

Probably talk about your feelings, do activities, and ask questions.

One question that I'm going to ask him is if people still have skin when they're in the ground.
Alex, the skin turns to dust and it doesn't hurt. I think that's a good question to ask. I bet the kids in the group have similar questions.

What if the kids in the group treat me differently?
Someone they loved also died. I can understand your being worried. We're all trying to find ways to cope with the loss of our special person. We are in mourning.

What's that?
Mourning is when people share their grief with friends and family. Lots of people might visit us this week. Every group of people, every culture, has their own way of mourning for the dead.

What do they do?
Some people cry in front of others. Some people pray. The funeral or cremation is a part of mourning. Mourning is a special time to remember Dad. What do you remember?

I remember the places in the house where he made me laugh, where we watched TV, and where he helped me with homework.
It's good to have so many memories of your dad.

I do have good memories of him, but I keep thinking that I could have done something to save him.
What do you think you could have done?

I should have talked to him before I went to school or stayed home that day. If I did, he wouldn't have killed himself. I did the wrong thing. I made a big mistake.
Dad was suffering from a disease. You had no idea that he was going to kill himself. You believe that you did the wrong thing,

but you didn't. You went to school as you should have. I was home with Dad and he still killed himself. You couldn't predict what Dad would do and neither could I.

Mom, do you forgive dad for killing himself?

He never should have taken his life.   But, I forgive him. He was ill.

Are you angry at Dad?

Alex, I'm angry at what your dad did. I'm angry by his act. I'm not angry at him.   I wrote him a letter telling him how angry I was at what he did, but that I loved him. You can also write him a letter and share your letter with me or anyone else. It feels good to write down what you're feeling. Writing feelings down will help you understand them. I don't have all the answers.

Yeah mom, I know you don't have all the answers, but talking does help. Praying helps too. When I pray, I feel like there's hope and when you have hope, you have everything.

Stop to Process

WHAT DID MY FAMILY DO WHEN WE WERE MOURNING?

LIST THE PEOPLE WHO I CAN TALK TO ABOUT MY SPECIAL PERSON'S SUICIDE.

DID PEOPLE IN MY FAMILY TALK ABOUT THE SUICIDE WITH EACH OTHER?

DID ANYTHING THEY SAID SCARE OR CONFUSE ME?

WHAT FEELING DO I HAVE ABOUT MY SPECIAL PERSON THAT I HAVE NOT SHARED WITH MY FAMILY?

WHAT IS MY BIGGEST PROBLEM RIGHT NOW?

HOW AM I WORKING OUT MY PROBLEM?

IF I CAN TELL A STORY ABOUT ANY LOSS AT ALL, WHAT WOULD IT BE?

HOW DO I FEEL AS I SHARE MY STORY?

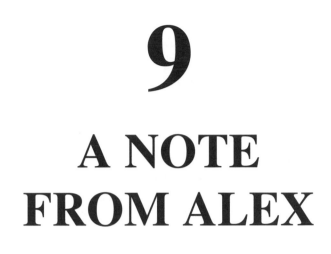

9

A NOTE
FROM ALEX

My mom said that we were grieving, but we were grieving together. Even though my dad died, we were still a family. And as a family we went to my dad's funeral. I had never been to a funeral before and had no idea what to expect. I think kids should decide if they want to go or not, but need to know from adults what they're like. My dad's body was buried at the funeral. It took place at a cemetery. After the funeral, our family went back to my house. One of things we did as a family was light a candle and say a prayer. It's important to only light candles when adults are with you. My sister and I would light our own candle after our mom lit hers. My mom then recited a poem. We did this a lot right after Dad died. Now we do it once a year on the anniversary of his death. My mom calls it "our ritual."

I remember one thing I did after my dad died was make a memory book of him. I put photographs of him in it. I also drew many pictures. One of the pictures I drew was of what I thought my dad's death looked like in the basement. I drew him holding a gun to his head. The gun was so big. It was bigger then his body. I also drew tears in his eyes. I showed the picture to my mom and we talked about what she saw after he died.

One of the things I did a few weeks after my dad died was make a collage. I cut out things from magazines my dad liked and glued them to a large sheet of paper. I also wrote a story about him. I drew a picture of a time machine, too. I imagined a time when my dad was alive. I even drew a picture of my family's wishing well and wrote down all my wishes. It was a neat picture. Mom and my sister also wrote down their wishes.

At first, I wished that I didn't have to go to the support group. But, looking back at it now, I am glad my mom told me to go. It really helped me understand what I was feeling. The kids in the group were nice. I liked drawing with them and talking to them. It made me realize that I wasn't the only one who had a special person die.   Some of the kids brought in things that belonged to their special person. I remember one girl wore the necklace of her mom, who died.

I still wear my dad's T-shirt and baseball cap. It feels good having stuff that belonged to my dad. I still have the note I wrote after he died. I let my grandma read the note and we talked about it. She told me stories about when he was a boy and brought me a photo album filled with pictures of him as a kid. It was so cool to see my dad and uncle Sammy as boys.

Grandma told me that I looked just like my dad in one of the pictures. That's the one that I took out of the album and kept on my table in my room. My room has changed since my dad died, five years ago. But, his picture is still on my table. Whatever death is, my dad would never be completely gone. My dad's dead, but he is still a big part of my life and always will be.

I was only ten when he died and really into baseball back then. It was hard not having him take me to the games, but the coach was a big help. I remember the coach took me to a practice a few days after the funeral. I thought everyone would be really weird. But no one on the team mentioned anything about it except for a few of my friends, who said they were sorry my dad died. I really missed my dad at the games. Every time I won a trophy I wished he was there. I think he somehow knows I won the trophies and is proud of me.

I just started taking karate. Is there something you're doing now that your special person would be proud of? Write about it! Think about things you did together. Share your memories and ask your questions. Even now, years after the death, I still ask questions, different ones, all the time. Sometimes I can't figure out the answers. Maybe you're thinking of the same questions or have different ones of your own.

I found some answers in the books that I have read written for kids who have lost a special person. In the beginning, it was hard to concentrate on anything. As time passed, it was easier to read and learn about what I was feeling. Some of the books had pages in them where I drew and wrote how I felt. I still have the workbooks and sometimes I look back on my pictures and notes. I think that my family, some of my friends, the support group I attended, prayer, and the stuff I read, really helped me cope with my dad's death. I hope this book, *But I Didn't Say Goodbye* helped you.

PART TWO

Bereavement Referrals

If a person saves a life, a single soul,
scripture imputes it to him or to her
as though he or she had saved alive
the whole world.
The Mishna

SUICIDE AWARENESS, PREVENTION & SURVIVOR SUPPORT

AMERICAN FOUNDATION FOR SUICIDE PREVENTION
120 Wall Street, 22nd Floor
New York, NY 10005
888-333-AFSP

The American Foundation for Suicide Prevention (AFSP) was founded in 1987 by a group of concerned scientists, business and community leaders, and survivors of suicide in an effort to support research and education needed to prevent suicide. AFSP remains the only national non-profit dedicated to funding suicide prevention research, and to providing initial support for investigators beginning their careers in this field.

The foundation has chapters nationwide which offer educational programs and conferences for survivors, mental health professionals, physicians, and the public to help raise awareness of the more than 30,000 suicides that occur in this country each year. AFSP believes that heightened awareness is vital in generating support for AFSP's efforts to prevent this needless tragedy from occurring in the future.

Call to order a copy of Fatal Mistakes: Families Shattered by Suicide, a 45 minute PBS documentary, produced and distributed by the American Foundation for Suicide Prevention, through an educational grant from Wyeth-Ayerst Laboratories.

SETTING UP A MEMORIAL FUND
There is a Hebrew word called tzedakah (tse-dah-kah). It means righteousness, to give of oneself to a noble cause. It's a way to honor the memory of the person who has died, whether from suicide, cancer, AIDS, heart disease, accident, or any type of death.

Friends and family can give tsedahkah in memory of the person who died and give of oneself to a noble cause. For example, an adult can set up a memorial fund with a not-for-profit, tax exempt organization dedicated to preventing suicide. The memorial fund honors the person who died, but also helps others. Children can also give tsedahkah and if not through money, they can donate time to help others. Adults and children can contribute to the memorial fund on the anniversary of the death, at birthdays or holidays, and make it a ritual.

Contributing each year to the memorial fund is a good way for children to be a part of a ritual. Donations provide support for research and offer a sense of comfort to both children and adult survivors. For further information on how one can make contributions, contact: The American Foundation for Suicide Prevention at 212-363-3500, Toll Free: 888-333-AFSP

FINDING A SUICIDE SURVIVOR SUPPORT GROUP

There are over 8 million survivors of suicide in the United States. The American Foundation for Suicide Prevention is continually adding new support groups to their directory on the web. For a suicide survivor support group in your area: http://www.afsp.org   888-333-AFSP

AMERICAN ASSOCIATION OF SUICIDOLOGY (AAS)

4201 Connecticut Avenue, NW
Suite 408, Washington, D.C. 20008
202-237-2280, Fax: 202-237-2282
Free AAS Survivor's Support Packet: Fact sheet, Coping Suggestions, Bibliography, 24 page booklet Resource Guide. *Surviving Suicide* Newsletter: Quarterly newsletter for and about survivors of suicide. Appropriate for survivors, support group leaders, and those who assist survivors.
Books: topics include coping with the loss of child or parent; caring for a child survivor; guidelines for starting and leading a support group for survivors; and suicide prevention books.
Membership: AAS welcomes and encourages survivors of

suicide to join the AAS survivors division. Benefits include: *Surviving Suicide* Newsletter, *Newslink* and Suicide and Life-Threatening Behavior (Official AAS publications), regular updates and mailings, and discounts on AAS books and conference registration fees.

Workshops & Conferences: AAS sponsors several educational and healing activities each year for survivors and those who counsel them. "Healing After Suicide" Conference provides opportunity for survivors to meet and network, share their stories, and provide support to one another.

FRIENDS FOR SURVIVAL, INC.
A National Resource for Families after a Suicide Death
P.O. Box 214463, Sacramento, CA 95821
Office/Fax: 916-392-0664
Suicide Loss Helpline: 800-646-7322
Friends For Survival, Inc. is a national non-profit organization open to those who have experienced a loss of family or friends by suicide and also to professionals who work with those who have been touched by a suicide tragedy. Friends for Survival, organized by and for survivors, has been offering services since 1983. All staff and volunteers have been directly impacted by a suicide death. They provide a variety of peer support services that comfort, encourage and educate those in grief. Friends for Survival, Inc. strives to increase community and national awareness of the impact of suicide

Offering: A monthly newsletter of support, information, and referral regarding local resources, Conferences and retreats, Comprehensive list of printed resources and tapes. Chapter development and training when local resources are absent. Collaboration with national efforts for suicide awareness. Suicide loss helpline with volunteers who have shared the tragedy of suicide

GRIEFWORK CENTER, INC.
P.O. BOX 5104
Kendall Park, NJ 08824
732-422-0400
Fax: 732-422-4609
e-mail: griefworkpress@aol.com
www.griefworkcenter.com

Griefwork Center, Inc. offers educational and professional training programs designed to give you the skills you need in responding in situations involving suicide. We provide staff in-service workshops and seminars across the U.S. that heighten awareness of the problem of suicide and the importance of postvention.

Caregivers responding In Situations Involving Suicide (C.R.I.S.I.S.) Model and Program: The critical component of the model approaches suicide as a public health problem. It is based on providing a structured framework of postvention exploring the fundamentals of the public's awareness of suicide and its aftereffects. The model promotes and supports the collaboration among community mental health and public health care providers, including law enforcement, clergy, media, funeral directors, educators, local government, physicians, nurses, emergency and medical services, suicide survivor support groups, parents and the public.

C.R.I.S.I.S. Postvention strategy:
Increasing public recognition of risk factors of suicide; Identifying the suicide survivor's unique grief, bereavement, and mourning; Offering concrete suggestions for helping child suicide survivors cope with their grief; Promoting informed portrayals of suicide in the media; Understanding the ways helping professionals can engender hope and support to survivors through the important alliance made with community resources; Providing a prompt transfer of recent developments in the field of suicidology research to community health care professionals; Burnout prevention for the professional care giver.

OASIS: ORGANIZATION FOR ATTEMPTERS AND SURVIVORS OF SUICIDE IN INTERFAITH SERVICES

45 Burlington Place, NW,
Washington, DC 20016
202-363-4224
Fax: 202-363-1468
e-mail: CTHV45A@prodigy.com

To enrich the lives of those who have been and will be touched by suicide. A systems approach to suicide awareness. They seek to fulfill their mission by increasing suicide awareness, removing stigma on attempters and survivors, facilitating educational programs, training professional caregivers and offering consultation and resources.

LIFEKEEPER FOUNDATION

"Dedicated To Suicide Prevention By Affirming Life"
3740 Crestcliff Court
Tucker, GA. 30084
678-937-9297
Fax: 678-937-9125
e-mail: lifekeeper@webmail.bellsouth.net

The Lifekeeper Foundation was formed by Sandy Martin in memory of her son Tony who died by suicide at age 17. It's purpose is suicide awareness, education, and prevention through art form such as Lifekeeper, jewelry, poetry and the National Memory Quilt. All proceeds are given to the various suicide prevention groups such as SPAN, LINK, AAS and AFSP.

The first displaying of the quilt was in April 1998 at the SPAN awareness event on the Capital steps in Washington D.C. Twenty-nine states and specialty groups were represented, and again later that year in October at SPAN's Advancing the National Strategy for Suicide Prevention. Their goal is to continue with these projects and to develop others as envisioned.

THE LINK'S NATIONAL RESOURCE CENTER
for Suicide Prevention and Aftercare (LINK, NRC)
348 Mt. Vernon Highway
Atlanta, GA 30328
404-256-9797
NRCLINK.ORG

The Link Counseling Center has been a national resource for survivors of suicide for over 20 years. Iris Bolton, the Executive Director of the Link, and author of My Son... My Son...; A Guide to Healing After Death, Loss, or Suicide, is internationally known for her work with survivors and her own inspirational   journey of healing following the suicide of her son in 1977. The LINK's National Resource Center, funded by a grant from the UPS Foundation, is focused on outreach. The NRC is dedicated to reaching out to those in need and connecting them to the resources available.

Free services for survivors who have lost a loved one by suicide include: Survivors Packet - describes unique aspects of grief following suicide, articles written by survivors of suicide, referral and support group information, and bibliography   Children's Grief Packet - articles concerning how to help children cope with death and children's grief bibliography   Library of grief literature Survivor newsletter, The Journey   Telephone counseling   Web site containing resource info.

Additionally, the NRC provides local support groups and crisis response for schools, business, places of worship, and anyone in the community needing support and guidance after a suicide. Members of The Survivors of Suicide Support Team, a group of trained survivors and mental health professionals, provide home visits for families and individuals following a self inflicted death. An annual SOS Support Team Training is held every fall in Atlanta.

The Link's NRC offers suicide prevention services including speeches and workshops on depression, the warning signs of suicide, and intervention methods. QPR training (Question Persuade Refer) is offered by certified instructors. Prevention resource materials are distributed nationally.

SA\VE
SUICIDE AWARENESS\VOICES OF EDUCATION
P.O. Box 24507
Minneapolis, MN 55424-0507
612-946-7998
http://www.save.org
The mission of SA\VE is to educate about the brain diseases that, if untreated medically and psychologically, can result in suicide death. To make statements by members' presence through events like the Annual Awareness Day, protest, letter writing or other activities. To honor the memory of people who died by suicide. To eliminate the stigma on suicide.

SA\VE was started in 1989 when five suicide survivors (people who have experienced the loss of a loved one to suicide) met and agreed on the need for an organization. SA\VE has expanded over the years and the present membership is about 300 active members and includes some other organizations that have common interests. The organization consists mostly of suicide survivors, but does include people that have suffered from depression. The major event for the organization is an Awareness Day held every spiring in Minneapolis, Minnesota.

Their website includes: information on symptoms/ danger signs, questions on suicide, depression facts, misconceptions on suicide, a loved one is suicidal, what to tell children, students and depression, elderly depression, book list with reviews, when the worst has happened, and starting a support group.

S.O.L.O.S., INC.
P.O. Box 1716
Springfield, VA 22151-0716
solos@1000deaths.com
A national organization committed exclusively to supporting Survivors of Loved Ones Suicide (SOLOS), studying their problems, developing new resources, meeting unmet needs, and educating the public and professionals about SOLOS.

SPAN   Suicide Prevention Advocacy Network
5034 Odin's Way
Marietta, GA 30068
888-649-1366
SPAN, a non profit, 501(C)3 organization dedicated to the creation of an effective national suicide prevention strategy. It bridges survivors with leaders in science, business, government, education and public health. Terri Ann Weyrach, M.D., died by suicide in June, 1987. Her parents founded SPAN in January, 1996. SPAN promoted US Senate Resolution 84, sponsored by Harry Reid, D-NV, declaring suicide a national problem and prevention a priority. The measure unanimously passed on May 6, 1997.

Collaborating with a cross-section of society, to create an effective National Suicide Prevention STRATEGY that will result in a sustained reduction in the number of suicides.

Educate Congress and the public to the current US near-epidemic nature of suicide. Develop and implement components of the STRATEGY in each state.

Acknowledges that no single suicide prevention program or effort will be appropriate for all populations or communities; encourages initiatives dedicated to preventing suicide; responding to people at risk for suicide and people who have attempted suicide; promoting safe and effective treatment for persons at risk for suicidal behavior; supporting people who have lost someone to suicide; and developing an effective national strategy for prevention of suicide.

Resolution encourages development, and promotion of accessibility and affordability of mental health services to enable all persons at risk for suicide to obtain the services without fear of any stigma.

SUICIDE INFORMATION & EDUCATION: CANADA

SIEC: SUICIDE   INFORMATION   &   EDUCATION CENTRE

#201, 1615 - 10th Avenue S.W.

Calgary, AB, Canada T3C 0J7

403-245-3900   Fax: 403-245-0299

e-mail: siec@siec.ca

www.siec.ca

The mission of the Suicide Information & Education Center (SIEC) is to assist educators, researchers, caregivers and the general public in their suicide prevention efforts through the acquisition and dissemination of information related to suicidal behavior.

The vision of SIEC is to have all persons apply knowledge and acquired skills to make healthy choices to resolve personal problems in a nonviolent manner. SIEC is a library and resource center which acquires published and unpublished documents and other resources related to suicide and suicidal behavior. The resources are indexed, abstracted and entered on a computerized database. The database is searchable by over 800 subject terms which are listed in the SIEC Thesaurus of Subject Terms, and hardcopy printouts are available.

Over 26,000 items are currently available and over 1,000 are added each year. Copies of most of the resources are available for research or study. The SIEC database is available on CD-ROM, or searches, documents and resources can be ordered on the Internet or by mail, phone or fax.

KING'S COLLEGE CENTRE FOR EDUCATION ABOUT DEATH AND BEREAVEMENT
266 Epworth Avenue
London, Ontario, N66A 2M3, Canada
519-432-7946
Fax: 519-432-0200
e-mail: jmorgan@julian.uwo.ca
http://www.wwdc.com/death

CANADIAN ASSOCIATION FOR SUICIDE PREVENTION
c/o The Support Network
#301, 11456 Jasper Avenue NW
Edmonton, Alberta T5K 0M1 Canada
780-482-0195
Fax: 780-488-1495
e-mail: casp@suicideprevention.ca
The Canadian Association for Suicide Prevention (CASP) was incorporated in 1985 by a group of professionals who saw the need to provide information and resources to the community at large to reduce the suicide rate and minimize the harmful consequences of suicidal behavior. Recently CASP has outlined its main purpose and function..
Vision: We, like many others, envision a world in which people enjoy an optimal quality of life, are long-living, socially responsible, and optimistic about the future.
Purpose: CASP's ultimate purpose is to reduce the suicide rate and minimize the harmful consequences of suicidal behavior.
Operation: CASP works toward the achievement of its purpose by facilitating, advocating, supporting, and advising, rather than by the provision of direct services.

DEATH EDUCATION & GRIEF COUNSELING

ADEC
ASSOCIATION FOR DEATH EDUCATION AND COUNSELING
638 Prospect Avenue
Hartford, CT 06105-4250
860-586-7503
Fax: 860-586-7550
e-mail: iadec@adec.org
www.adec.org
ADEC is the oldest interdisciplinary organization in the field of dying, death, and bereavement.
ADEC promotes and shares research, theories, and practice in dying, death, and bereavement.
ADEC offers opportunities for those of like interests to share knowledge and exchange ideas with the goal to improve the way in which our society deals with grief, dying, and death.
ADEC is a tax-exempt, non-profit organization.
ADEC puts these services to work for you: Journals, Newsletter, Annual Conference, Certification, Professional Recognition, Directory of Members, Professional Development. Learning Resource Directory, Chapters and International Networking, and Special Interest Groups.

ALIVE ALONE
Bi-monthly newsletter for parents now childless. Help bereaved parents network.
Contact Kay and Rodney Bevington
11115 Dull Robinson Road
Van Wert, OH 4589
419-238-1091

AMERICAN HOSPICE FOUNDATION
130 Connecticut Avenue
NW Suite 700
Washington, DC 20036-4101
202-223-0204
Fax: 202-223-0208
Offers on-site training workshops for managers, employee assistance professionals, educators, bereavement counselors, and mental health professionals.

THE CENTER FOR LOSS AND GRIEF THERAPY
Linda Goldman
10400 Connecticut Avenue
Suite 514
Kensington, MD 20895
301-942-6440,
e-mail: Lgold@erols.com
www.erols.com/lgold
Linda Goldman, MS. LPC, Certified Grief Therapist has a private practice where she works with children, teenagers, families, and grieving adults. Linda gives workshops, courses, and trainings on children and grief.

Books by Linda Grollman:
(1998). Bart speaks out: Breaking the silence on suicide. Los Angeles: CA. Western Psychological Services at 1-800-648-8857.
(1996). Breaking the silence: A guide to help children with complicated grief: Suicide, homicide, AIDS, violence and abuse. Muncie, IN: Accelerated Development at 1-800-821-8312
(2000). Life & Loss: A guide to help grieving children, 2nd. ed. Accelerated Development.

THE CENTER FOR LOSS AND LIFE TRANSITION

3737 Broken Bow Rd.
Fort Collins, CO 80526
970- 226-6050
Fax : 970- 226-6051

e-mail: wolfelt@centerforloss.com

The Center for Loss and Life Transition, Directed by Dr. Alan Wolfelt, is dedicated to furthering our understanding of the complex emotions we call grief. Their mission is to help both the bereaved, by walking with them in their unique life journeys, and bereavement caregivers, by serving as an educational liaison and professional forum. Contact the Center for their catalog of Wolfelt publications, a catalog of training courses, and their on-line newsletter.

THE COMPASSIONATE FRIENDS

http://compassionatefriends.org/index.html

The mission of The Compassionate Friends is to assist families in the positive resolution of grief following the death of a child and to provide information to help others be supportive. The Compassionate Friends is a national nonprofit, self-help support organization which offers friendship and understanding to families who are grieving the death of a child of any age, from any cause. There is no religious affiliation. There are no membership fees or dues, and all bereaved family members are welcome.

THE DOUGY CENTER
The National Center for Grieving Children & Families
3909 SE 52nd Avenue
PO Box 86852
Portland, OR 97286
503- 775-5683
Fax: 503-777-3097
www.dougy.org
The Dougy Center provides loving support where grieving children, teens and their families share their experience as they move through their healing process. The Dougy Center, a 501(c)3 non profit organization, extends supportive services to the family, caregivers, schools, businesses and the community.

Offering   guidebooks, videos and other resource material, the National Directory of Children's Grief Services, and program development training at their center in Portland. Contact the Dougy Center, The National Center for Grieving Children and Families to order their guidebook, *Helping children cope with death.* (1997).

HOPE FOR BEREAVED, INC.
A Bereavement Support Organization
4500 Onondaga Blvd.
Syracuse, NY 13219
Business: 315-475-9675
Fax: 315- 475-3298
Helpline listening, counseling, referrals: 315-475-HOPE
Directory of bereavement and training programs include HOPE's nationally recognized book, HOPE FOR BEREAVED: Understanding, Coping and Growing Through Grief, books for youth, 'Unexpected Death At School' packets, Grief in the Workplace Training Program, Bereavement Caregivers Conference, and more.

HOSPICE FOUNDATION OF AMERICA
2001 Street, Suite 300
Washington, DC 20009
202-638-5419   Fax: 202-638-5312
www.hospicefoundation.org
Hospice produces *Journeys*, a monthly newsletter on grief and bereavement. Provides information and guidance to companies on handling grief in the workplace and offers the "Living with Grief" teleconference series, which provides free bereavement education and assistance to over 100,000 professionals and lay people annually throughout North America.

IN LOVING MEMORY
1416 Green Run Lane
Reston, VA   20190
703-435-0608   Fax: 703- 435-3111
Eastern Standard Time:10am-9pm
A non-profit organization eligible to receive tax deductible contributions created to support bereaved parents who have suffered the death of their only child or all of their children.

LARGO
Quarterly newsletter for parents who have had more than one child die, is published by Sascha Wagner
1192 S. Uvalda Street
Aurora, CO   80012
303-745-1799

NEW ENGLAND CENTER FOR LOSS & TRANSITION
A non profit organization
P.O. Box 292
Guilford, CT 06437-0292
203-458-1734
e-mail: staff@neclt.org.   www.neclt.org

CRISES INTERVENTION

NATIONAL HOPE LINE NETWORK
Help is just a phone call away. If you or someone you know is contemplating suicide call National Hope Line Network.
800-SUICIDE

BOYS TOWN NATIONAL HOTLINE
800-448-3000

EMERGENCY INFORMATION
Call 911 if you are seeking emergency help for someone who is exhibiting violent behavior, or who may harm himself, herself or someone else.

AAS SUICIDE PREVENTION/CRISIS INTERVENTION CENTERS DIRECTORY
Contact information for more than 750 agencies in U.S. and Canada. $18.00 (includes shipping and handling).

ADDICTIONS

ALCOHOLICS ANONYMOUS
212-685-1110

NARCOTICS ANONYMOUS
800-352-3792

CAMPS FOR GRIEVING CHILDREN

AMERICAN HOSPICE FOUNDATION
800-658-8898

CAMP JAMIE
Sponsored by the Hospice of Frederick County. Camp Jamie is a special weekend camp for grieving children ages 6-24.
516 Trail Avenue
Frederick, MD 21702
301-698-3030

CAMP NEW HOPE
Sponsored by Delaware Hospice in Dover, DE
call 302-678-4444 for various locations

INFORMATION ON DEPRESSION

NATIONAL ALLIANCE FOR THE MENTALLY ILL
200 N Glebe Rd., Suite 1015
Arlington, VA 22203-3754
800-950-6264

NATIONAL FOUNDATION FOR DEPRESSIVE ILLNESS, INC.
PO Box 2257, New York, NY 10116
800-248-4344

NATIONAL DEPRESSIVE AND MANIC DEPRESSIVE ASSOCIATION
730 N Franklin St., Suite 501
Chicago, IL 60610
800-826-3632

ANXIETY DISORDERS ASSOCIATION OF AMERICA
6000 Executive Blvd., Suite 513
Rockville, MD 20852
301-231-9350

SUICIDOLOGY WEBSITES

http://psychcentral.com/helpme.htm
Suicide Resources on the Internet

http://www.yellowribbon.org
Light for Life Foundation

http://www.sfsuicide.org
San Francisco Suicide Prevention

http://www.lollie.com/suicide.html
A Comprehensive Approach to Suicide Prevention

http://www.uke.uni-hamburg.de/ens
European Network for Suicidology(ENS)

The websites lised on the previous page will take you to other important sites on the Internet. Use this page to note links for future reference.

APPENDIX A

RECOMMENDED RESOURCES

Children speak from spirit.
There is great wisdom
in a child suicide survivor's voice.
Listen, and they will teach you much.
-Barbara Rubel

MAGAZINES, NEWSLETTERS & REPORTS

BEREAVEMENT PUBLISHING, INC.
A Magazine of Hope and Healing
5125 N. Union, Suite 4
Colorado Springs, CO 80918
888-604-HOPE

THE FORUM NEWSLETTER
Association for Death Education and Counseling (ADEC)
638 Prospect Avenue,   Hartford, CT 06105-4250

THE SURGEON GENERAL'S CALL TO ACTION TO PREVENT SUICIDE 1999
Department of Health and Human Services
U.S. Public Health Service
www.surgeongeneral.gov
On July 28, 1999, Tippor Gore and Surgeon General David
Satcher hosted a press conference at which the Surgeon General
announced a blueprint to prevent suicide in the United States.
The document outlines steps that can be taken by individuals,
communities, organizations and policy makers. A copy of the
Surgeon General's Call To Action may be obtained from the
Office of the Surgeon General's web site or by contacting SPAN.

THE THANATOLOGY NEWSLETTER
Brooklyn College
Dept. of Health & Nutrition Sciences, Editorial Office
Brooklyn, NY 11210-2889

RENEWAL NEWSLETTER
National Center for Death Education
Mount Ida College
777 Dedham Street
Newton Center, MA 02159

MAIL ORDER BOOKS, VIDEOS & AUDIO TAPES

"FATAL MISTAKES: FAMILIES SHATTERED BY SUICIDE" chronicles the recovery of several survivors in the aftermath of suicide including Barbara Rubel, author of *But I Didn't Say Goodbye*.

The Documentary, produced and distributed by the American Foundation for Suicide Prevention (AFSP), also includes interviews with several of America's leading researchers and clinicians on the latest advances and trends in suicide prevention research featuring Dr. David Clark, Dr. Jan Fawcett, Dr. Fred Goodwin, Dr. Kay Redfield Jamison, Dr. John Mann, Dr. Alex Roy, and Dr. David Shaffer.

Produced by Kingsley Communications and narrated by Mariette Hartley, Fatal Mistakes is an award winning television documentary that educates viewers about suicide's impact on survivors and the latest advances in prevention. It was honored with a Regional Emmy Award for its PBS broadcast in the Houston, TX. Area, the Golden Eagle awarded by the Council on International Non-theatrical Events, (CINE), and a bronze medal at the New York Film Festival in health and medical category. This award-winning documentary received two prestigious honors in 1998, the Silver Hugo Award-the highest honor presented by the International Communication Film and Video Competition, and the Columbus International Film Video Festival's first place award in the Health category.

Suggested Audiences: Survivor support groups, survivor conferences, mental health professionals, guidance counselors, clergy, social workers, employee assistance professionals, and general public.

Price (includes shipping and literature): $19.99

To order: 888-333-AFSP

or 212-363-3500

AQUARIUS
Health Care Videos in Harmony with the Heart
5 Powderhouse Lane
PO Box 1159
Sherborn, MA 01770
508-651-2963
Fax: 508-650-4216
e-mail aqvideos@tiac.net   www.aquariusproductions.com
Bereavement Videos from the leader in health care related video productions. Newsletter for professionals in bereavement and healing published four times a year. Subscription for one year is $19.95. Call for a free copy.
Before You Say Good-bye: An eye-opening wake-up call documenting the startling reality of suicide. 1998, 30 minutes
Beyond Death's Door, 1999, 30 minutes
Kids to Kids: When someone special dies, 1999, 12 minutes
Living with Loss Healing with Hope: Compiled from Rev. Earl Grollman, international expert on grief. 1995, 12 minutes
No easy way: Coping with a loved One's Suicide. 1998, 30 min.
Saying Goodbye/Teens: Teens sharing their stories of grief and loss, per two video set, 1994, 34 & 37 minutes
The Tomorrow's Children Face When A Parent Dies: Children sharing their insights and feelings. 1997, 47 minutes
What Do I tell My Children: For families and professionals who are dealing with children and grief issues. 1991, 30 minutes

BOULDEN PUBLISHING
P.O. Box 1186
Weaverville, CA 96093-1186
800-238-8433
Fax: 530-623-5525
www.bouldenpub.com
Interactive Bereavement Counseling Resources for Today's Youth: Audio tapes, video tapes, CD-Roms, and books
Award of excellence - National Hospice Organization, *Saying Goodbye"* is used by 15,000 schools and hospices.

CENTERING CORPORATION

1531 North Saddlecreek Road
Omaha, NE 68107
402-553-1200
Fax: 402-553-0507
e-mail: J1200@aol.com

Centering is a non-profit bereavement resource center. The Centering Corporation was founded in 1977 by Joy and Dr. Marvin Johnson. They have over 300 books, videos and other resources related to grief. Call today for their Creative Care Package.

Joy and Dr. Marvin Johnson are nationally known speakers and writers.

Recommended Videos: Children Grieve Too, $39.00; Standing Tall Teen Grief, $39.00; I am a Survivor - Suicide families speak out $39.00

KIDSPEACE FULLFILLMENT DEPT.

1650 Broadway
Bethlehem, PA 18015-3998
1-800-8KID-123

VHS and CD ROM: "Children Grieve, Too!"

A three hour seminar of practical clinical advice, proven methods and successful applications. Linda Goldman was videotaped live on location at the National Hospital 17th National Conference. "Children Grieve, Too!" is available in two formats:

VHS (3 tape set). The three tape set includes: Part One: What is children's Grief; Part Two: Helping the grieving child in the school; Part Three: Children and complicated grief.

Also available in CD ROM (Not MAC compatible). Add this important presentation to your professional resources library.

$150.00 each plus $5.00 s/h

COMPASSION BOOKS
477 Hannah Branch Rd.
Burnsville, NC 28714
828-675-5909
24 Hour Fax: 828-675-9687
www.compassionbooks.com
The world's largest mail-order collection! Over 400 carefully
selected books, audios and videos on death and dying,
bereavement and change, comfort, healing, inspiration and
hope... collected from hundreds of publishers. Resources to help
people grow through loss and change. Donna O'Toole, M.A. the
director and founder of Compassion Books is available as a
conference leader or trainer.

MENTAL HEALTH RESOURCES
346 West Saugerties Road
Saugerties, NY 12477
914-247-0116
Fax: 914-247-9189
e-mail: mhr@ulster.net

BRUNNER/MAZEL
A MEMBER OF THE TAYLOR & FRANCIS GROUP
47 Runway Road
Levittown, PA 19057
800-821-8312
Fax: 215-269-0363
e-mail: bkorders@taylorandfrancis.com
Essential reading for Death Educators, Traumatologists, and
Grief Counselors

HOWARD ROSENTHAL SUICIDE PREVENTION AUDIO TAPES
To order call Taylor and Francis 1-800-821-8312
For Young People - 30 min.
Crash Course for Counselors and Therapists - 30 min.

BOOKS FOR ADULT SURVIVORS

Aarons, L. (1995). Prayers for Bobby: A mother's coming to terms with the suicide of her gay son. San Francisco: Harper Collins.

Alexander, V. (1998). In the wake of suicide: Stories of the people left behind. San Francisco: Josey Bass.

Baugher, R. , & Calija, M. (1998). A guide for the bereaved survivor: A list of reactions, suggestions, and steps for coping with grief. Newcastle, WA: Author.

Bolton, I., & Mitchell, C. (1983). My son...my son.... A guide to healing after a suicide in the family. Atlanta, GA: Bolton Press.

Collins, J. (1998). Singing Lessons: A memoir of love, loss, hope, and healing. NY: Pocket Books.

Dalke, D. (1994). If daddy loved me, why did he leave me? For parents and families caring for children after one parent has committed suicide. Omaha, NE: Centering Corporation.

Derrek, K. (1995). Dancing with the skeleton: Meditations for suicide survivors. Omaha, NE: Centering.

Fine, C. (1997). No time to say goodbye: Surviving the suicide of a loved one. NY: Doubleday.

Fitzgerald, H. (1992). The grieving child: A parent's guide. NY: Simon and Shuster.

Fitzgerald, H. (1995). The mourning handbook. NY: Simon and Shuster.

Gilbert, R. (1999). Finding your way after your parent dies: Hope for grieving adults.   Notre Dame, IN: Ave Marie Press.

Golden, T.R. (1996). Swallowed by a snake: The gift of the masculine side of healing. MD: Golden Healing Publishing.

Goodwin, B.R. (1996). The best little girl says goodbye: A therapist grieves. Bethel, CT: Rutledge Books.

Hammer, S. (1991). By her own hand: Memories of a suicide's daughter. NY: Soho Press.

Kaplan, S., & Lang, G. (1995). Grief's courageous journey: A workbook. Oakland, CA: New Harbinger Publications, Inc.

Lockridge, L. (1994). Shade of the raintree: The life and death of Ross Lockridge, Jr. NY: Viking.

Puryear, A. (1997). Stephen lives: My son Stephen: His life, suicide and afterlife. NY: Pocket Books.

Rando, T. (1988). How to go on living when someone you love dies. NY: Bantam Books.

Ross, E.B. (1990). After suicide: A ray of hope. Iowa City, IA: Lynn Publishers.

Sanders, C.M. (1992). Surviving grief . . . and learning to live again. NY: John Wiley & Sons, Inc.

Sexton-Jones, S. (1996). This is survivable. When someone you love completes suicide. Omaha, NE: Centering Corporation.

Steel, D. (1998). His bright light: The story of Nick Traina. NY: Delacorte Press.

Vanderbilt, G. (1997). A mother's story. NY: Plume.

Wrobleski, A. (1994). Suicide Survivors: A guide for those left behind. (2nd ed.). Minneapolis, MN: Afterwards Publishing.

ADULT BOOKS ON CREATIVITY & WRITING TO HEAL

Reading poems that acknowledge grief and offer supportive insight may plant seeds for a person to write when the time is ripe. John Fox believes that for some people, trauma may catalyze their need to express. Poem making will feel from the very beginning an essential part of getting through what feels unspeakable. People who have never written a poem in their life may find that poems come to them and flow without having to think about it. Writing poetry may help you or your client, friend, child or loved one cope by providing emotional release, self-care and insight on the difficult journey of living with loss.

Fox, J. (1995). Finding what you didn't lose: Expressing your truth and creativity through poem-making. New York: Tarcher/Putnam.

Fox, J. (1997). Poetic medicine: The healing art of poem-making. New York: Tarcher/Putnam.

BOOKS FOR PROFESSIONALS

Alexander, V. (1998). In the wake of suicide: Stories of the people left behind. San Francisco: Jossey-Bass.

Brooks, B., & Siegel, P. M. (1996). The scared child. New York: John Wiley & Sons, Inc.

Cimbolic, P. & Jobes, D.A. (1990). Youth suicide: Issues, assessment, and intervention. Ill: Charles Thomas Publisher, Ltd.

Clark, D. (Ed.). (1993). Clergy response to suicidal persons. Chicago: Exploration Press.

Cook, A.S., & D.S. Dworkin (1992). Helping the bereaved:

Therapeutic interventions for children, adolescents, and adults. USA:
Basic Books.

Corr, C., & Corr, D. (1996). Handbook of childhood death and
bereavement. New York: Springer.

Corr, C., & Balk, D.(1996). Handbook of adolescent death and
bereavement. New York: Springer.

Crow, G.A. & Crow, L.I. (1997). Helping parents cope with
children's adjustment problems: An advice-giving guide for
professionals. ILL:Charles Thomas Publisher, Ltd.

Doka, K. (1989). Disenfranchised grief. Lexington, MA:
Lexington Books.

Doka, K. (Ed.) (1995). Children mourning, mourning children.
Bristol, PA: Taylor & Francis.

Doka, K.J. (Ed.). (1996). Living with grief after sudden loss:
Suicide, homicide, accident, heart attack, stroke. Bristol, PA:
Taylor & Francis.

Doka, K.J., & Davidson, J.D. (Eds.). (1998) Living with grief:
Who we are, how we grieve. Philadelphia, PA: Brunner/Mazel.

Ellis, T.E. & Newman, C.F. (1996). Choosing to live: How to
defeat suicide through cognitive therapy. CA: New Harbinger.

Gilbert, R. (1996). Heartpeace: Healing help for grieving folks.
St. Meinrad, IN: Abbey Press.

Gilbert, R. (1997). Responding to grief: A complete resource
guide. Point Richmond, CA : Spirit of health.

Goldman, L. (1994). Life & loss: A guide to help grieving children.
Muncie: IN: Accelerated Development.

Goldman, L. (2000). Breaking the silence: A guide to help children with complicated grief: Suicide, homicide, AIDS, violence and abuse. (2nd. ed.). Muncie: IN: Accelerated Development.

Grollman, E. A. (1990). Talking about death: A dialogue between parent and child (3rd ed.). Boston: Beacon Press.

Grollman, E.A. (1990). Suicide: Prevention, intervention and postvention. Boston: Beacon Press.

Grollman, E. A. (1995). Bereaved children and teens: A support guide for parents and professionals. Boston: Beacon Press.

Hendin, H. (1995). Suicide in America (2nd ed.). New York: W.W. Norton and Company.

Jacobs, D.G. (Ed.). (1999). The Harvard Medical School guide to suicide assessment and intervention. San Francisco: Jossey-Bass.

Jamison Redfield, K. (1999). Night falls fast: Understanding suicide. NY:Knopf.

Kleespies, P., (Ed.). (1997). Emergencies in mental health practice: Evaluation and management. NY:Guilford.

Lester, D. (1992). Why people kill themselves: A 1990's summary of research findings on suicidal behavior. (3rd ed.). ILL: Charles Thomas Publisher, Ltd.

Lester, D. (1993). The cruelest death: The enigma of adolescent suicide. Philadelphia, PA: The Charles Press.

Lester, D., & Tallmer, M. (Eds.). (1994). Now I lay me down: Suicide in the elderly. Philadelphia, PA: The Charles Press.

Lester, D. (1997). Making sense of suicide: An in-depth look at why people kill themselves. Philadelphia: The Charles Press.

Maris, R.W., Silverman, M.M., & Canetto, S. S. (Eds.). (1997). Review of suicidology, 1997. New York: The Guilford.

McIntosh, J.L., Santos, J.F., Hubbard, R.W., & Overholser, J.C. (1994). Elder suicide: Research, theory, and treatment. Hyattsville: MD. American Psychological Association.

Miller, J. (Ed.). (1992). On suicide: Great writers on the ultimate question. San Francisco: Chronicle Books.

Mishara, B. L. (Ed.). (1995). The impact of suicide. New York: Springer.

Pritchard, C. (1995). Suicide - The ultimate rejection? A psycho-social study. Buckingham, UK: Open University Press.

Rando, T., (1993). Treatment of complicated mourning. Champaign, IL: Research Press.

Redfield Jamison, K. (1997). An unquiet mind. NY: Random House.

Redfield Jamison, K. (1999). Night falls fast: Understanding suicide. NY:Knopf.

Rickgarn, R.L.V. (1994). Perspectives on college student suicide. Amityville, NY: Baywood.

Shneidman, E.S. (1985). Definition of suicide. New York: Wiley.

Shneidman, E.S. (1995). The psychology of suicide: A clinician's guide to evaluation and treatment. (Rev. ed.). Northvale, NJ: Jason Aronson.

Shneidman, E. (1996). The suicidal mind. New York: Oxford University Press.

Silverman, P.R. & Nickman, S. L. (1996). Continuing bonds: New understands of grief. Washington, DC: Taylor & Francis.

Slaby, A. & Garfinkel, L.F. (1996). No one saw my pain: Why teens kill themselves. NY: W.W. Norton & Company.

Smith, S.C., & Pennells, M. (Eds.). (1995). Interventions with bereaved children. Bristol, PA: Jessica Kingsley.

Stroebe, M.S., Stroebe, W., & Hansson, R.O. (1997). Handbook of bereavement: Theory, research, and intervention. United Kingdom: Cambridge University Press.

Wolfet, A. (1983). Helping children cope with grief. Bristol, PA: Taylor & Francis.

Wolfelt, A.D.(1996). Healing the bereaved child: Grief gardening, growth through grief and other touchstones for caregivers. Ft. Collins, CO: Companion Press.

Worden, J. W. (1991). Grief counseling and grief therapy. (2nd ed.). New York: Springer.

SUICIDE PREVENTION BOOKS

Berman, A.L., & Jobes, D.A. (1997). Adolescent suicide: Assessment and intervention. Washington DC: American Psychological Association.

Capuzzi, D., & Golden, L.B. (1988). Preventing adolescent suicide. Muncie, IN: Accelerated Development.

Clark, D. (Ed.). (1993). Clergy response to suicidal persons and their family members. Chicago: Exploration Press.

Shneidman, E. (1985). The definition of suicide. New York: John Wiley & Sons & Sons.

Williams, K. (1995). A parent's guide for suicidal and depressed teens: Help for recognizing if a child is in crisis and what to do about it. Center City, MN: Hazelden Foundation.

JOURNALS FOR PROFESSIONALS

ARCHIVES OF SUICIDE RESEARCH: OFFICIAL JOURNAL OF THE INTERNATIONAL ACADEMY FOR SUICIDE RESEARCH
Kluwer Academic Publishers
P.O. Box 358, Accord Station Hingham, MA 02018-0358

CRISIS: THE JOURNAL OF CRISIS INTERVENTION AND SUICIDE PREVENTION
Published under the Auspices of the International Association for Suicide Prevention (IASP)
Hogrefe & Huber Publishers
P.O. Box 2487, Kirkland, WA 98083-2487

DEATH STUDIES
Taylor & Francis Subscriptions office
47 Runway Road, Suite G, Levittown, PA 19057-4700
215-269-0400   Fax: 215-269-0363

GRIEF MATTERS
THE AUSTRALIAN JOURNAL OF GRIEF AND
BEREAVEMENT
The Centre for Grief Education
P.O.Box 1569
Clayton South VIC 3169, Australia
Tel. 612-9545-6377   e-mail: griefmatters@grief.org.au
(Payment must be in Austrailian dollars and may be made by
check or credit card (Mastercard/Visa)

THE HOSPICE JOURNAL
The Hayworth Press, Inc.
10 Alice Street
Binghamton, NY 13904-1580
607- 722-5857

ILLNESS CRISIS & LOSS
SAGE Publications, Inc.
2455 Teller Road
Thousand Oaks, CA 91320
805- 499-0721

JOURNAL OF PERSONAL & INTERPERSONAL LOSS
Taylor & Francis
1900 Frost Road, Suite 101, Bristol, PA 19007
215-785-5800   Fax: 215-785-5515

OMEGA JOURNAL OF DEATH AND DYING
Baywood Publishing Company
26 Austin Avenue, Amityville, New York 11701
800- 638-7819

SUICIDE AND LIFE-THREATENING BEHAVIOR
THE OFFICIAL JOURNAL OF THE AMERICAN ASSOCIATION
OF SUICIDOLOGY
GUILFORD PUBLICATIONS, INC.
Dept. 7L, 72 Spring Street
New York, NY 10012
800-365-7006 or 212-431-9800

BOOKS FOR CHILDREN

Adler, C.S. (1993). Daddy's climbing tree. New York: Clarion Books.

Buscaglia, L. (1982). The fall of Freddie the leaf: A story of life for all ages. Thorofare, NJ: Charles B. Slack.

Goldman, L. (1998). Bart speaks out: Breaking the silence on suicide. Los Angeles, CA: Western Psychological Services.

Goldman, L. (1996). Breaking the silence: A guide to help children with complicated grief: Suicide, homicide, AIDS, violence and abuse. Muncie, IN: Accelerated Development

Goldman, L. (2000). Life & Loss: A guide to help grieving children, (2nd. ed.). Accelerated Development

Hanson, W. (1997). The next place. Minneapolis, Minnesota: Waldman House.

Harris, L. & Dawson, S. (1999). Jack's journey. Wilmore, KY: Words on the Wind.

Liss-Levinson, N. (1995). When a grandparent dies. Woodstock, Vermont: Jewish Lights Publishing.

Richmond, Judy. (1998). <u>Just you and me.</u> St. Joseph, MO: Hands of Hope Hospice.

Salloum, A. (1998). <u>Reactions: A workbook to help young people who are experiencing trauma and grief</u>. Omaha, NE: Centering Corporation.

Spelman, C. (1996). <u>After Charlotte's mom died</u>. Morton Grove, IL: Albert Whitman.

Traisman, E.S. (1994). <u>Remember: A child remembers</u>. Omaha, NE: Centering Corporation.

BOOKS FOR TEENAGERS

Gootman, M. (1994). <u>When a friend dies: A book for teens about grieving & healing.</u> Minneapolis, MN: Free Spirit.

Grollman, E. A. (1993). <u>Straight talk about death for teenagers</u>. Boston, MA: Beacon Press.

Grollman, E.A., & Malikow, M. (1999). <u>Living when a young friend commits suicide: Or even starts talking about it.</u> Boston: Beacon Press.

Nelson, R.E. & Galas, J.C. (1994). <u>The power to prevent suicide.</u> Nubbeaoikusm MN: Free Spirit Publishing.

Stevenson, L.C. (1990). <u>Happily after all</u>. Boston: Houghton Mifflin Company.

Traisman, E. (1992). <u>Fire in my heart, ice in my veins: A journal for teenagers</u>. Omaha, NE: Centering Corporation.

CRISIS IN THE SCHOOLS: RESOURCES FOR EDUCATORS

Aldrich, L. M. (1996) Sudden Death: Crisis in the school. Cherry Hill, NJ: Author.

Cassini, J., & Rogers, L. (1996). Death and the classroom. Burnsville, NC: Compassion Books.

Fairchild, T. N. (1997). Crisis intervention strategies for school-based helpers (2nd ed.). Springfield, IL: Charles C. Thomas.

Fitzgerald, H. (1998). Grief at school. Washington, DC: American Hospice Foundation.

Gliko-Braden, M. (1992). Grief comes to class. Omaha, NE: Centering Corporation.

Grief at school: A guide for teachers and counselors. (1996). Brochure can be ordered through the American Hospice A teacher's guide to the grieving student: Guidelines and suggestions for school personnel grades K - 12. (1995). PA: Hospice of Lancaster County.

Helping the Grieving student: A guide for teachers. (1998). Portland, OR: The Dougy Center for Grieving Children

Kirk, W.G. (1993). Adolescent Suicide: A school-based approach to assessment and intervention. Champaign, IL: Research Press.

Stevenson, R. (1997). What will we do? Preparing a school community to cope with crisis. Amityville, NY: Baywood Publishing Co.

Team up to save lives: What every school should know about suicide. (1996). Institute for Juvenile resources. A CD for Schools. 1-800-627-7646.

Underwood, M. M., & Dunne-Maxim, K. (1992) Managing sudden traumatic loss in the schools. Piscataway, NJ: University of Medicine and Dentistry of New Jersey

ARTICLES OF INTEREST

Appleby, L., Amos. T., Doyle, U., Tomenson, B., & Woodman, M. (1996). General practitioners and young suicides: A preventive role for primary care. British Journal of Psychiatry, 168, 330-333.

Berman A. L., and Jobes D. A. (1995), Suicide prevention in adolescents (age 12-18). Suicide and Life-Threatening Behavior, 25, 143-154.

Centers for Disease Control and Prevention. (1995). Suicide among children, adolescents, and young adults-United States, 1980-1992. MMWR, 44 289-291.

Cox, G.R. (2000). Children, spirituality, and loss. Illness, Crisis & Loss, 8, 1. 60-70.

Farberow, N.L. (1992, Summer). Grief and Mourning After Suicide, Lifesavers, 4, 5.

Firestone, R.W., & Firestone, L. (1998). Voices in suicide: The relationship between self-destructive thought processes, maladaptive behavior and self-destructive manifestations. Death Studies 22, 411-443.

Grossman, J., Hirsch, J., Goldenberg, D., Libby, S., Fendrich, M., Mackesy-Amiti, M.E., Mazur, D., & Chance, G.H. (1995). Strategies for school-based response to loss: Proactive training and postvention consultation. Crisis, 16, 18-26.

Gunnell, D., & Frankel, S. (1994), Prevention of suicide: Aspirations and evidence. British Medical Journal 308, 1227-1233.

Hazell, P. & Lewin, T. (1993), An evaluation of postvention following adolescent suicide. Suicide and Life-Threatening Behavior, 23, 101-109.

Jamison, K. R. (1994, Summers). Suicide and manic-depressive illness. Lifesavers, 6, 4-5, 7.

Kachur, S.P., Potter, L.B., James, S.P., Powell, K.E. (1995). Suicide in the United States, 1980-1992. Violence Surveillance Summary, No.1. Atlanta, GA: Centers for Disease Control and Prevention, National Center for Injury Prevention and Control.

Kelly, J. (1997, October). The Grief Process - A cognitive equilibrium model in adapting to loss Paper presented at the meeting of the Canadian Association for Suicide Prevention Thunder Bay, ON.

Leenaars, A.A., & Wenckstern, S. (1999). Suicide prevention in schools: The art, the issues, and the pitfalls. Crisis, 20, 132-142.

Lipschitz, A. (1995), Suicide prevention in young adults (age 18-30). Suicide and Life-Threatening Behavior, 25, 155-170.

Malone, K., & Mann, J. J. (1995, Summer) Serotonin and the Suicidal Brain. Lifesavers, 7, 4-5.

Mazza, J.J., & Reynolds, W.M. (1998). A longitudinal investigation of depression, hopelessness, social support, and major and minor life events and their relation to suicidal ideation in adolescents. Suicide and Life-Threatening Behavior 28, 4. 358-374.

Pfeffer, C. (1991, Summer). Suicide Survivors. Lifesavers, 3, 3.

Potter, L.B., Powell, K.P., & Kachur, S.P. (1995). Suicide prevention from a public health perspective. Suicide and Life Threatening Behavior, 25, 82-91.

Provini, C., & Everett, J.R., & Pfeffer, C.R. (2000). Adults mourning suicide: Self-reported concerns about bereavement, needs for assistance, and help-seeking behavior. Death Studies, 24, 1. 1-19.

Rihmer, Z. (1996), Strategies of suicide prevention: Focus on health care. Journal of Affective Disorders 39, 83-91.

Rubel, B. (1995, September). Suicide survivors: The journey of grief. Visions Magazine, 12-13, 34.

Rubel, B. (February-May, 1996). Suicide and Healergy. [On line]. Available: http://www.castle.net~mystic.

Rubel, B. (1996, Summer). My three sons' gift: A survivor story. Lifesavers, 8, 4-5.

Rubel, B. (1996, Fall). Dealing with panic, anxiety and stress during the grief process. Panic Relief News, 8, 7.

Rubel, B. (1996, November/December). Suicide...The portrait of grief. The Forum, 9.

Rubel, B. (1996). Suicide risk to recovery. The Recovery Link, 2, 21.

Rubel, B. (1999). Impact of a grief-crisis intervention immediately after a sudden violent death on the survivor's ability to cope. Illness, Crisis & Loss, 7, 4. 391-404.

Rubel, B. (1999) Reducing the risk of suicide ideation by managing pain and treating underlying depression. Illness, Crisis & Loss, 7, 4. 325-332.

Rubel, B. (1999). The grief-response experienced by the survivors of suicide. The Thanatology Newsletter, 6, 1. 8-10.

Rubel, B. (1999, July). [Review of the book My brother Peter: Murder or suicide? Thirty years later, a sister's quest for peace and the truth] The Thanatology Newsletter, 6, 2. 20-21.

Rubin, S.S. (1999). The two-track model of bereavement: Overview, retrospect, and prospect. Death Studies, 23, 681-714.

Satcher, D. (1998). Bringing the public health approach to the problem of suicide. Suicide and Life-Threatening Behavior 28(4), 325-327.

Silverman, M. M., & Felner, R. D. (1995), The place of suicide prevention in the spectrum of intervention: Definitions of critical terms and constructs. Suicide and Life-Threatening Behavior 25(1), 70-81.

Tomori, M. (1999). Suicide risk in high school students in Slovenia. Crisis, 20, 23-27

Wheeler, S.R., & Austin, J. (2000). The loss response list: A tool for measuring adolescent grief responses. Death Studies, 24, 1. 21-34.

Wilcox, H. C., & Shaffer, D. (1996, Spring). The Columbia Teen Screen Suicide Prevention Project. Lifesavers. 9, 2-3, 9-10.

INSPIRATIONAL SELECTIONS

Brener, A. (1994). Mourning and Mitzvah: A guided journal for walking the mourner's path through grief to healing. Woodstock, VT: Jewish Lights Publishing.

Flynn, J. (1994). A little talk with God. Louisville: Accord.

Gambil, A. (1997). Food for the soul: A best of bereavement poetry collection. Colorado Springs: Bereavement Publishing.

Gilbert, R. (1996). Heartpeace: Healing help for grieving folks. St. Meinrad: Abbey Press.

Magida, A.J., & Matlins, S.M. & Cloud, Jr. S. (Eds.). (1997). How to be a perfect stranger: A guide to etiquette in other people's religious ceremonies. (vol. 2). Woodstock: Jewish Lights.

Miller, J. E. (1995). A pilgrimage through grief: Healing the soul's hurt after loss. St. Meinrad: Abbey Press.

Mundy, L. (1996). What helps the most when hope is hard to find: 101 insights from people who have been there. St. Meinrad: Abbey Press.

O'Brien, M. (1997). Praying through grief: Healing prayer services for those who mourn. Notre Dame, IN: Ave Maria Press.

Sims, D. (1996). If I could just see hope. Wenatchee: Big A & Co.
For additional spiritual resources, contact the Rev. Dr. Richard B. Gilbert, The World Pastoral Care Center, 1504 N. Campbell Street, Valparaiso, IN 46385-3454. 219-464-8183, fax: 219-531-2230, e-mail: rgilbert@valpo.edu

MEN AND GRIEF

Doka, K. (1998). Grief beyond gender: Understanding the ways men and women grieve. Philadelphia, PA: Brunner/Mazel.

Golden, T.R. (1996). Swallowed by a snake: The gift of the masculine side of healing. Kensington, MD: Golden Healing Publishing.

Levang, E. (1998). When men grieve: Why men grieve differently and how you can help. Minneapolis, MN: Fairview Press.

Martin, T., & Doka, K.J. (1999). Men don't cry . . . women do: Transcending gender stereotypes of grief. Philadelphia, PA: Brunner/Mazel.

Miller, J.E., & Golden, T. (1998). When a man faces grief: Twelve practical ideas to help you heal from loss. Fort Wayne, IN: Willowgreen Publishing.

Miller, R., & Hrycyniak, S.J. (1999). Griefquest: Men coping with loss. Winona, MN: St. Mary's Pr.

Mundy, L., & Alley, R.W. (1998). Grief therapy for men. St. Meinrad, IN: Abbey Press.

Staudacher, C. (1991). Men and grief : A guide for men surviving the death of a loved one. Oakland, CA: New Harbinger Pub.

HUMOR AND HEALING

Holden, R. (1999). Laughter the best medicine: The healing powers of happiness, humour and joy. New York: J.P. Tarcher.

Klein, A. (1998). <u>The courage to laugh: Humor, hope and healing in the face of death and dying.</u> New York: J.P. Tarcher.

Obershaw, R.J. (1998). <u>Cry until you laugh: Comforting guidance for coping with grief</u>. Minneapolis: MN: Fairview Pr.

COPING DURING THE HOLIDAYS

Miller, J.E. <u>How will I get through the holidays? 12 ideas for those whose loved one has died</u>. (1996). Fort Wayne, IN: Willowgreen.

Smith, H. I. <u>A Decembered Grief: Living with loss while others are celebrating</u>. (1999). Beacon Hill Press.

GRIEF PRODUCTS ON INTERNET

Grief Resources Catalog by Grief Encounters, Inc.
5021 Vernon Avenue, #209, Edina, MN 55436
Phone or Fax: 612-922-3469, www.griefresourcescatalog.com
Order grief products from Internet catalog. Over 100 different items including books, cards, tapes and gifts .

MEMORIAL SONGS AND MUSIC
Benefiting Suicide Prevention

Before Their Time Volume 1- www.beforetheir time.com or phone 888-216-7611 toll free in U.S. and Canada; A collection of memorial music in memory of people who died young. A musical resource to promote healing. CD $15.00; cassettes $10, plus $3. for s/h, All net revenue benefits Hospice VNH (VT/NH) and NH Youth Suicide Prevention Assn.

NOTES

QUICK ORDER FORM

Please complete information or tape business card here

Name:

Institution:

Address:

City/State:

Zipcode:

Phone/e-mail:

fax:

Please send me_____copies of But I Didn't Say Goodbye
by Barbara Rubel, ISBN #1-892906-00-7
$14.95 each plus $3.00 shipping.
For each additional book ordered, add $1.00 shipping.
Check/money order enclosed: $ _____

Make checks payable to: Griefwork Center, Inc.

Terms: Orders must be prepaid by check or money order.
New Jersey residents add applicable sales tax.

Canada: All Canadian orders must be prepaid with a check in
U.S. funds/U.S. bank. As required by law, applicable Canadian
GST apply. Shipping slightly higher outside U.S.A.

Please send FREE information on:

Griefwork Center, Inc. Support Packet for persons who survive
the suicide of someone close to them _____

Caregivers Responding In Situations Involving Suicide
(C.R.I.S.I.S.) Model and Program_____

Suicide Statistics _____

Risk Factors that help dispel the myths of suicide_____

Griefwork Center, Inc.
P.O. Box 5104, Kendall Park, NJ 08824
Mon. - Fri., 9 AM-5 PM EST
call: 732-422-0400
fax: 732-422-4609   e-mail: griefworkpress@aol.com
visit our website: http://www.griefworkcenter.com
For photos of book and author for publication reproduction,
please contact Griefwork Center, Inc.